THE *APOLLO 11* SPACECRAFT

Columbia Command Module (CM)

Contains crew's living area, flight controls, forward and rear control jets, reentry heat shields, and para-chutes for splashdown. Has a docking system for locking onto the lunar module.

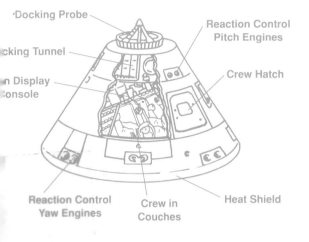

Docking Probe

Reaction Control Pitch Engines

cking Tunnel

Crew Hatch

n Display onsole

Reaction Control Yaw Engines

Crew in Couches

Heat Shield

Eagle Lunar Module (LM)

A two-stage vehicle that can carry two astronauts to and from the moon. The descent stage contains the rocket engine, fuel tanks, and legs for landing. The ascent stage contains the crew compartment, windows, and controls and an engine for independent flight. The two stages act as one vehicle until the ascent stage separates during lunar liftoff to reunite with *Columbia*.

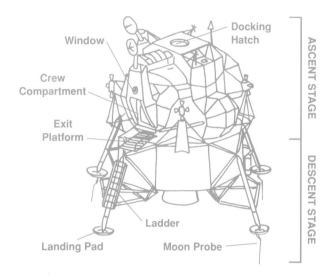

Window

Docking Hatch

Crew Compartment

Exit Platform

ASCENT STAGE

DESCENT STAGE

Ladder

Landing Pad

Moon Probe

Service Module (SM)

Apollo 11 spacecraft's electrical power supply and main rocket, with a thrust of 20,500 pou

Spacecraft ~~apter~~ (SLA)

...as and landing gear are folded down while stowed in the protective adapter.

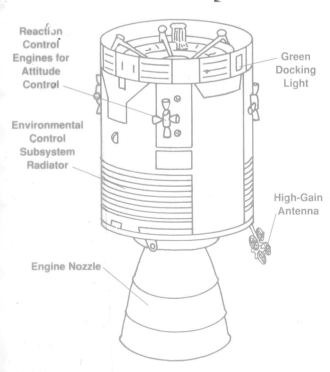

Reaction Control Engines for Attitude Control

Green Docking Light

Environmental Control Subsystem Radiator

High-Gain Antenna

Engine Nozzle

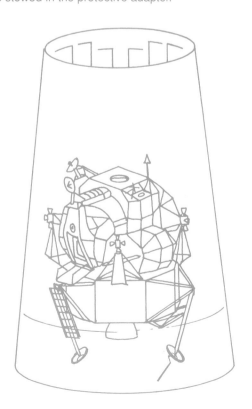

THE MOON

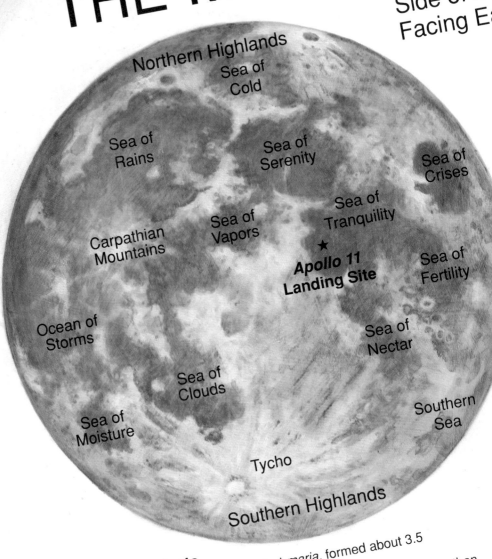

Northern Highlands

Sea of
Cold

Sea of
Rains

Sea of
Serenity

Sea of
Crises

Sea of
Tranquility

Carpathian
Mountains

Sea of
Vapors

★
**Apollo 11
Landing Site**

Sea of
Fertility

Ocean of
Storms

Sea of
Nectar

Sea of
Clouds

Southern
Sea

Sea of
Moisture

Tycho

Southern Highlands

Moon Facts
–Dark, low-level areas, called *maria*, formed about 3.5 billion years ago.
–Light areas, called *highlands*, are more rugged and older than the dark areas.
–The diameter of the moon is about one-fourth that of the earth.
–The average distance from the moon to the earth is 240,000 miles.
–A person who weighs 100 pounds on the earth weighs 17 pounds on the moon.
–The moon has no air, water, or living things.
–Looking out from the moon, the sky is always black because there is no air to scatter sunlight.

ONE GIANT LEAP

WRITTEN AND ILLUSTRATED BY
MARY ANN FRASER

Henry Holt and Company ● New York

Moon Phases

NEW

WAXING CRESCENT

FIRST QUARTER

WAXING GIBBOUS

FULL

WANING GIBBOUS

LAST QUARTER

WANING CRESCENT

View from Earth

Henry Holt and Company, Inc.
Publishers since 1866
115 West 18th Street
New York, New York 10011

Henry Holt is a registered
trademark of Henry Holt and Company, Inc.

Published in Canada by Fitzhenry & Whiteside Ltd.,
91 Granton Drive, Richmond Hill, Ontario L4B 2N5.

Library of Congress Cataloging-in-Publication Data
Fraser, Mary Ann.
One giant leap / written and illustrated by Mary Ann Fraser.
Summary: A moment-by-moment re-creation of the first space flight
to the moon, culminating in Neil Armstrong's step onto its surface.
1. Project Apollo (U.S.)—Juvenile literature.   2. Space flight to
the moon—Juvenile literature.   [1. Project Apollo (U.S.)   2. Space
flight to the moon.]   I. Title.
TL789.8.U6A5336   1993
629.45'4'0973—dc20   92-41044

ISBN 0-8050-2295-3

First Edition—1993

Printed in the United States of America on acid-free paper.∞

1   3   5   7   9   10   8   6   4   2

All quotes come from the NASA *Apollo 11*
technical air-to-ground voice transcripts
and *Apollo 11 Moon Landing,* by David
J. Shayler (London: Ian Allan Ltd, 1989).

Acknowledgments

Special thanks to the staff of the Rice University Library, Ken Bornsley of the
Kennedy Space Center Public Affairs Office, and Joey Kuhlman of the NASA
Johnson Space Center History Office for their willingness to provide photo-
graphs and transcripts and to answer my many questions.

Dedication

To Alexander, for his inspiring curiosity, and to
the three astronauts of *Apollo 11:* Edwin E. Aldrin, Jr.,
Neil A. Armstrong, and Michael Collins.

July 16, 1969

For thousands of years people have explored the earth, from mountaintops to ocean floors, but travel to the moon was no more than a dream—until, that is, July 16, 1969. On that morning at Cape Kennedy, Florida, the three astronauts of the *Apollo 11* moon mission prepared to travel a quarter of a million miles into space. If all went well, one of them would be the first person to step onto the moon.

One at a time Neil Armstrong, Buzz Aldrin, and Michael Collins squeezed through the hatch of the spacecraft that would be their home for the next eight days. The computer-filled *Apollo* spacecraft and the three-stage *Saturn V* rocket on which it perched had taken more than 300,000 people eight years to plan, test, and build. It was the largest and most powerful space vehicle ever constructed.

GROUND ELAPSED TIME*

Hours   Minutes Seconds

-002:28:11

*Time from Launch

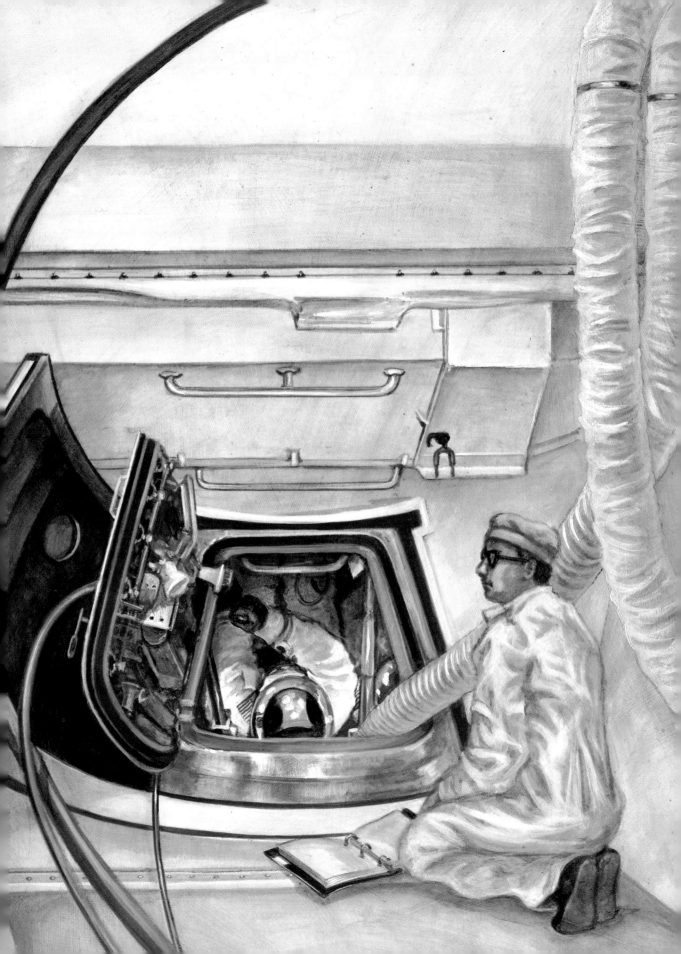

GROUND ELAPSED TIME*

Hours   Minutes   Seconds

*Launch occurred at 9:32 A.M. EST

While their families anxiously awaited liftoff, the astronauts listened to a voice at Apollo-Saturn launch control count off the last ten seconds. T-minus "10...9..." The five huge engines of the rocket's first stage exploded into flames as 8,000 gallons of water per minute gushed onto the launchpad to cool it. "8...7...6...5..." All five engines were now up to 90 percent of their power, clouds of steam and smoke billowed about the rocket, and the astronauts could hear the fuel tanks sloshing and feel the engines swiveling to keep the rocket upright. "4...3...2...1...0! All engines running!" The hold-down clamps swung back. "Lift off!...we have a liftoff." The towering space vehicle cleared the launchpad and arced over the Atlantic Ocean, leaving a trail of fire. Mission Control in Houston took over ground command.

Some of the nearly two million spectators at Cocoa Beach cheered and clapped, while others watched in silence. The rocket pierced the white wispy clouds, rose above Earth's atmosphere, and plunged into the darkness of space.

Two-and-a-half minutes into the flight the astronauts lurched forward against their straps. The *Saturn V*'s first stage had shut down and fallen away into the Atlantic Ocean. Four seconds later the second stage erupted into flames and slammed the crew back into their seats. As that stage used the last of its fuel and separated from the command and service modules, the men pitched violently forward once again. The astronauts were now weightless.

Lieutenant Colonel Michael Collins, a 38-year-old former test pilot, sat in the right-side couch. He was the command-module pilot.

Together the command module and service module were called *Columbia,* after the explorer Christopher Columbus. The cone-shaped command module that housed the astronauts was the main control center for the *Apollo 11* spacecraft. It had a protective cover and was latched to the top of the service unit. The cylindrical service unit carried fuel, food, and oxygen.

GROUND ELAPSED TIME

Hours   Minutes Seconds

000:09:12

On the center couch was 39-year-old Colonel Edwin E. "Buzz" Aldrin, Jr., a veteran of many jet missions during the Korean War. His job was to pilot the lunar module, *Eagle,* when it carried Neil Armstrong and himself from the command module to the moon and back again.

Strapped into the left-side couch was 38-year-old Neil A. Armstrong, commander of the *Apollo 11* mission. He was also an experienced pilot who had served in the Korean War. Even as a child he had loved flight and had built a wind tunnel in his parents' basement to test his model airplanes.

GROUND ELAPSED TIME

Hours   Minutes   Seconds

002:44:15

Now *Saturn V*'s third and final stage fired. The spacecraft entered a circular orbit around Earth. The crew checked equipment and secured all floating objects.

For the first time the space travelers could look back and marvel at their home planet. It glistened like a giant marble colored white by the clouds, rusty red by the deserts, and blue by the sparkling oceans.

After one-and-a-half orbits, the third stage ignited again. The *Apollo* spacecraft tore from orbit and ripped through space faster than a bullet through a rifle barrel. It was aimed at a point in the sky where the moon would be in three days.

The crew switched seats for their next flight maneuver. Collins fired the jets around the outside of the service module. Gradually *Columbia* separated from *Eagle*, which was snug in its protective shell between the service module and the third stage.

Now Collins pushed the computer key to turn *Columbia* around from its launch position and reattach it to *Eagle* for its flight position.

GROUND ELAPSED TIME

Hours   Minutes Seconds

004:10:30

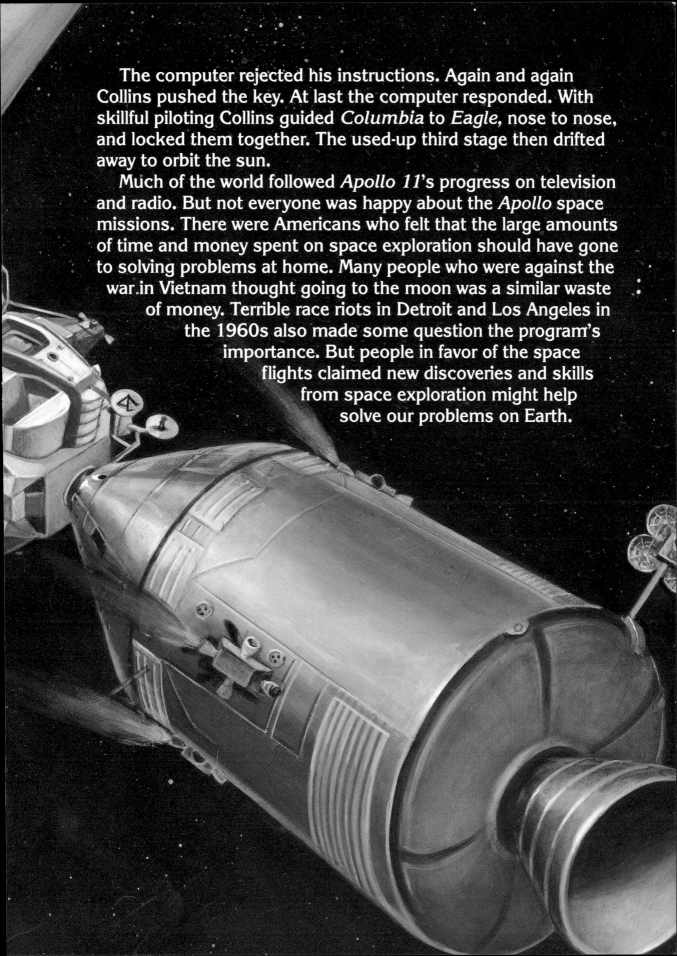

The computer rejected his instructions. Again and again Collins pushed the key. At last the computer responded. With skillful piloting Collins guided *Columbia* to *Eagle*, nose to nose, and locked them together. The used-up third stage then drifted away to orbit the sun.

Much of the world followed *Apollo 11*'s progress on television and radio. But not everyone was happy about the *Apollo* space missions. There were Americans who felt that the large amounts of time and money spent on space exploration should have gone to solving problems at home. Many people who were against the war in Vietnam thought going to the moon was a similar waste of money. Terrible race riots in Detroit and Los Angeles in the 1960s also made some question the program's importance. But people in favor of the space flights claimed new discoveries and skills from space exploration might help solve our problems on Earth.

For the first two days after leaving Earth's orbit, the spacecraft sped toward the moon, continually rotating to keep the fuel tanks from overheating and the radiators from freezing. Toward the sun was constant light and heat; away from the sun was cold, empty darkness dotted with stars.

The crew spent their time checking equipment, eating, cleaning, and conducting regular telecasts to Earth. They also received news from home, including progress reports of the unmanned Soviet *Luna 15*. This robot explorer was designed to bring back the first soil and rocks from the moon, beating out the Americans.

Many people saw the space program as a competition among nations, a contest the United States had been losing. The Soviets had put *Sputnik*, the first satellite, into space in 1957, and then Yuri Gagarin, the first human into orbit around Earth, in 1961.

That same year President John F. Kennedy promised that the United States would land a person on the moon by the end of the decade. Only eight years later, *Apollo 11* had completed the first lap in the space race to the moon.

GROUND ELAPSED TIME

Hours   Minutes   Seconds

007:10:14

July 19, 1969

On the fourth morning of the mission the astronauts woke to a spectacular view of the moon that filled three-quarters of the hatch window. Soon preparations were under way for the dangerous task ahead.

Mission Control reviewed the mission's status with the astronauts. "This is Apollo Control at 75 hours into the mission. *Apollo 11* is 2,241 nautical miles away from the moon. Velocity, 5,512 feet per second. . . . We're 41 minutes away from loss of signal as *11* goes behind the moon."

Radio signals to and from Earth cannot bend around the moon, which meant the astronauts would be out of contact whenever they circled to the moon's back side. Time passed slowly for the men of Mission Control, who waited patiently for news from *Apollo 11*.

GROUND ELAPSED TIME

Hours   Minutes Seconds

The astronauts had to fire the spacecraft's engine, a step they called engine burn, to slow down and be captured by the moon's gravity. If the rocket failed to fire, *Apollo 11* would loop around the moon and head back to Earth. If the rocket fired for too long, *Apollo 11* would crash into the moon's surface.

Finally the spacecraft "came over the hill."

"*Apollo 11, Apollo 11,* this is Houston. How do you read? . . . Could you repeat your burn status report?"

"Reading you loud and clear, Houston," replied Armstrong. "It was like—like perfect!"

All of *Apollo 11*'s journey to this point had been made before by previous Apollo missions; only the unknown lay ahead.

GROUND ELAPSED TIME

Hours   Minutes   Seconds

100:13:00

July 20, 1969

As the sun rose in Houston, Mission Control gently woke the crew. *"Apollo 11, Apollo 11*—good morning from the Black Team."

Michael Collins replied, "Good morning, Houston . . . oh my, you guys wake up early."

The astronauts may not have been ready to wake up, but this was the day they had waited and trained for: landing day. After breakfast and a briefing from Mission Control, Aldrin and Armstrong put on their liquid-cooling undergarments. Grabbing hold of the handrails, they floated into *Eagle*. Collins remained behind so he could help his fellow astronauts if anything went wrong.

On *Apollo 11*'s thirteenth orbit, Collins pushed the switch to release the final latches. Gently the modules drifted apart to become two independent vehicles.

Houston broke through the static as *Eagle* soared from behind the moon. "Roger. How does it look?"

Armstrong was now controlling *Eagle*. He answered, *"Eagle* has wings."

GROUND ELAPSED TIME

Hours   Minutes Seconds

102:33:22

One-and-a-half hours later tension mounted again as *Eagle* followed *Columbia* toward the back side of the moon to begin its descent. In less than 11 minutes Armstrong and Aldrin had to cross 300 miles of the moon's surface in *Eagle*, dropping in a long curve from 50,000 feet to touchdown.

Any equipment failure or miscalculation would mean turning back or certain disaster. If a leg on the lunar module came to rest on a boulder or slope and the module toppled over, *Eagle* would not be able to take off. The men would be stranded. Some scientists thought that the moon's windless surface had a dangerously deep coating of dust. They worried that the module or men would sink into this loose lunar soil.

Back on Earth, hundreds of journalists packed newsrooms while millions of TV viewers and radio listeners tuned in for word of the astronauts. The people of Mission Control waited for the static on their headsets to clear.

Eagle swung around from behind the moon, heading for the landing site on the Sea of Tranquility. Armstrong's voice finally came through. "The burn was on time."

"Current altitude about 46,000 feet, continuing to descend," reported the flight controller in Houston.

Just then ground control lost direct communication with *Eagle*. All commands had to be relayed through Mike Collins in *Columbia*. Armstrong adjusted *Eagle*'s position in flight, and Mission Control tried again to communicate directly. "*Eagle*, Houston. You are go. Take it all at four minutes. Roger, you are go—you are go to continue power descent."

"Roger." Aldrin had heard the message and commented, "And the earth right out our front window."

Suddenly an alarm went off in the cabin. "Twelve-o-two—twelve-o-two!" shouted Armstrong. "Give us the reading on the twelve-o-two program alarm."

GROUND ELAPSED TIME

Hours   Minutes   Seconds

The guidance computer was overloaded with data, but Mission Control decided *Eagle* should still proceed with landing. "Roger . . . we got—we're go on that alarm."

Armstrong peered through his small, triangular window. The computer was taking them to a stadium-size crater littered with ancient boulders, rock, and rubble. With the flip of a switch, Armstrong seized full manual control from the computer. Now he had to use all the flying skills he had learned as a pilot.

He adjusted the spacecraft's hovering position while Aldrin guided him. "Lights on. Forward. Good. Forty feet, down two and a half. Picking up some dust. Thirty feet, two and a half down. Faint shadow. Four forward. Four forward, drifting to the right a little." The rocket's firing was creating dust clouds, making it difficult to see.

Armstrong frantically searched for a site. Mission Control interrupted, "30 SECONDS!" Only 30 seconds of fuel for landing remained. Armstrong had to land immediately.

GROUND ELAPSED TIME

Hours   Minutes   Seconds

102:45:41

Slowly he lowered the craft. The blue light in the cockpit flashed. "Contact light," reported Aldrin. One of the three probes, like a feeler on a giant insect, had touched ground. "Okay, engine stop." They had landed four miles west of their original target, but still within the planned area.

"Houston, Tranquility Base here. The *Eagle* has landed," said Armstrong.

"Roger, Tranquility, we copy you on the ground," replied Mission Control. "You've got a bunch of guys about to turn blue. We're breathing again. Thanks a lot."

Back on Earth people of all nationalities celebrated the moon landing. But while Americans Armstrong and Aldrin had been skillfully piloting their spacecraft toward the Sea of Tranquility, *Luna 15* had crashed into the moon's Sea of Crises at nearly 300 miles per hour.

For several seconds Aldrin and Armstrong, the first humans on the moon, waited for the dust to settle about their spacecraft. Slowly they got their first glimpse of an alien world that had not changed for millions of years.

Meanwhile Collins in *Columbia* orbited to the back side of the moon, totally on his own for the first time.

A billion people from all over the world anxiously waited for the first steps onto the moon. Aldrin and Armstrong were no longer being viewed as Americans, but as representatives of all humanity.

GROUND ELAPSED TIME

Hours   Minutes   Seconds

109:14:00

GROUND ELAPSED TIME
Hours   Minutes Seconds
109:23:15

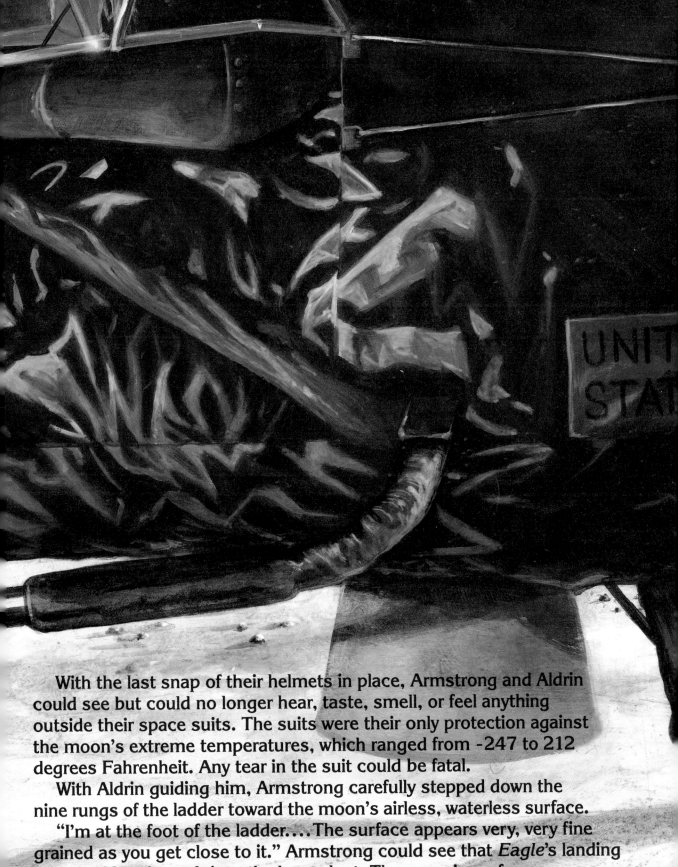

With the last snap of their helmets in place, Armstrong and Aldrin could see but could no longer hear, taste, smell, or feel anything outside their space suits. The suits were their only protection against the moon's extreme temperatures, which ranged from -247 to 212 degrees Fahrenheit. Any tear in the suit could be fatal.

With Aldrin guiding him, Armstrong carefully stepped down the nine rungs of the ladder toward the moon's airless, waterless surface.

"I'm at the foot of the ladder.... The surface appears very, very fine grained as you get close to it." Armstrong could see that *Eagle*'s landing pads had barely sunk into the lunar dust. The moon's surface seemed safe. "I'm going to step off the LM [lunar module] now."

Exactly 109 hours, 24 minutes and 15 seconds into the mission, Armstrong stepped off the landing pad and placed the first human footprint on the moon.

"That's one small step for man, one giant leap for mankind," he said.

He had meant to say, "one small step for *a* man," but in his excitement and nervousness he left out the *a*. A few moments later Aldrin joined him.

With those first prints in the lunar dust the people of Earth proved they could reach beyond their planet and touch the moon. Neil Armstrong, Buzz Aldrin, and Michael Collins, through skill, courage, and teamwork, had helped realize centuries of dreams. Other men and women could now follow in their footsteps.

Beyond the First Steps

While on the lunar surface, Armstrong and Aldrin began to answer the many questions we have about the history of our moon and solar system. They conducted an experiment designed to catch gas particles from the sun—solar wind—and they set up a device for measuring meteoroid impacts and "moonquakes." They also brought back samples of the moon's surface to be studied.

When their work was completed, the two astronauts blasted off in the top half of *Eagle* and rejoined *Columbia*. After 21 hours and 37 minutes visiting the moon, the space explorers headed for home.

On Thursday, July 24, 1969, Michael Collins, Neil Armstrong, and Buzz Aldrin safely splashed down in the Pacific Ocean, their mission accomplished.

Landing on the moon is considered by many to be humanity's greatest scientific achievement. The flight of *Apollo 11* was the first step in the exploration of other planets and solar systems; it was a triumph of the ageless human need to investigate the unknown. But it was also part of the space race between the United States and the Soviet Union for power on Earth. While the moon remains much the same as when *Apollo 11* left it, life on this planet has changed quickly.

Since the 1989 collapse of the Soviet Union, the long and frightening competition between that nation and the United States to conquer space and gain world power has ended. At the same time the American government has had less and less money available for expensive space projects. The horrible explosion that killed seven astronauts and destroyed the space shuttle *Challenger* also made many people wonder how safe space flight really is. For now, retrievable spacecraft and unmanned probes will take the lead in space exploration.

SPLASHDOWN

Hours   Minutes   Seconds

195:17:52

USSR A-1 Sputnik (1957)

USA Vanguard (1958)

USA Juno 1 (1958)

USA Thor-Agena (1959)

USSR A-2e Mars/Venus (1961)

USA Mercury-Redstone (1961)

The world is also facing difficult challenges such as AIDS, famine, and ecological destruction. No single nation has the money, technology, and time both to solve its own problems and to set off into space. But the urge to explore still remains. As we dream and plan for journeys to Mars and beyond, we are finding that cooperation is achieving what competition can no longer inspire.

International teamwork for space exploration is already in progress. Canada built the robot arm of the space shuttles, Japan conducted experiments aboard the space shuttle *Endeavor,* Italy has agreed to build sections of the space station *Freedom,* and the president of the United States has approved the use of Russian rockets to launch American commercial satellites.

Despite our national differences of language and customs, *Apollo 11* demonstrated that there is at least one thing we all share. Perhaps Buzz Aldrin summed it up best during a telecast following his return to Earth. He said, "We've come to the conclusion that this has been far more than three men on a voyage to the moon, more still than the efforts of a government and industry team, more even than the efforts of a nation. We feel that this stands as a symbol of the insatiable curiosity of all mankind to explore the unknown."

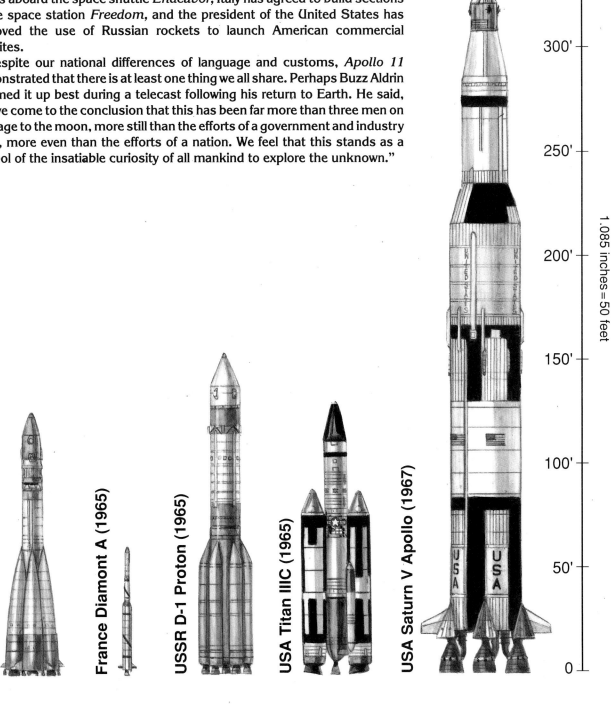

USSR A-1 Vostok (1961)

France Diamont A (1965)

USSR D-1 Proton (1965)

USA Titan IIIC (1965)

USA Saturn V Apollo (1967)

400'

350'

300'

250'

200'

150'

100'

50'

0

1.085 inches = 50 feet

GLOSSARY

Black Team: Apollo had four teams of flight controllers, each with a different shift: the Green Team, the White Team, the Maroon Team, and the Black Team.

Cape Kennedy: Launch complex in Florida, originally called Cape Canaveral. Its name was changed to Cape Kennedy shortly after President John F. Kennedy's assassination in 1963 and then back to Cape Canaveral in 1973.

docking: Connecting two or more objects in space.

engine burn: To fire an engine.

gravity: A force with which an object attracts another object; for example, the force with which a planet pulls on objects. The larger the planet, the greater the pulling force.

hover: To remain above a place or an object.

lunar: Of or referring to the moon.

module: A self-contained unit of a spacecraft designed to perform a specific job.

orbit: To circle an object.

reentry: The return of a space vehicle or object to the earth's atmosphere.

solar wind: Gases given off by the sun.

Soviet Union: Founded in 1917 out of the Russian empire, this communist state was the largest country in the world, covering one-sixth of the globe's surface.

space race: The competition among nations to lead in space exploration.

thermal: Of or relating to heat.

thrust: The force caused by firing a rocket engine.

wind tunnel: A tunnel that air is blown through to study the effects of wind on an object. It is often used to test how well something flies.

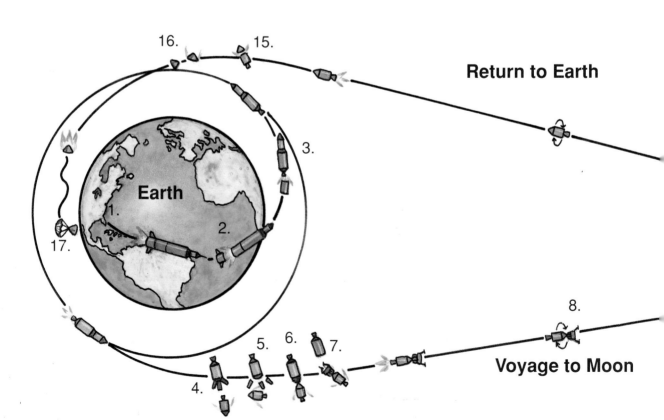